staffordsh errier

understanding and
caring for your breed

Written by
Clare L

12634029

staffordshire bull terrier

understanding and
caring for your breed

Written by
Clare Lee

Pet Book Publishing Company

The Old Hen House, St Martin's Farm, Zeals, BA12 6NZ, United Kingdom.

881 Harmony Road, Unit A, Eatonton, GA31024 United States of America.

Printed and bound in China through Printworks International.

All rights reserved. No part of this work may be reproduced, in any form or by any means, electronic or mechanical, including photocopying, recording or by any information storage and retrieval system, without the prior written permission of the publisher.

Copyright © Pet Book Publishing Company 2012

Every reasonable care has been taken in the compilation of this publication. The Publisher and Author cannot accept liability for any loss, damage, injury or death resulting from the keeping of Staffordshire Bull Terriers by user(s) of this publication, or from the use of any materials, equipment, methods or information recommended in this publication or from any errors or omissions that may be found in the text of this publication or that may occur at a future date, except as expressly provided by law.

The 'he' pronoun is used throughout this book instead of the rather impersonal 'it', however no gender bias is intended.

ISBN: 978-1-906305-63-5
ISBN: 1-906305-63-3

Acknowledgements

The publishers would like to thank the following for help with photography: Steve Halifax, Sharon Pearse and Steve Horsman (Bullhawk), Andy Jones (Gwynford), Clare Lee (Constones), JoAnn Essex (Javawolf), Shirley Gray (Bullmaple), Jum Beaufoy (Wyrefare), and Bill & Jo Blacker (Crossguns).

Contents

Introducing the Staffordshire Bull Terrier

The Staffordshire Bull Terrier is a dog of medium size, strongly built, with well- developed muscles, a broad head, a short coat and a fine, whippy tail. He has a very extrovert character.

The Stafford cannot be missed powering down the street, usually at the end of his lead. Meeting him in his home, he will be effusively friendly. He craves attention and will sit closely beside you to allow easier patting and stroking. Meet him at the park and he may well be chasing, hell for leather, to catch a ball or a frisbee. He is a picture of energy, a powerhouse in compact housing.

The Stafford is a very smart dog, well capable of thinking for himself. Staffords are also outstandingly

good at overcoming and forgetting bad experiences which is the basis for their cheerful, stable, and fearless temperament.

Low maintenance

The Staffordshire Bull Terrier is a medium-sized dog, with a short easy-to-care-for coat. He is physically very strong and, as a breed, they suffer from few hereditary problems. Our vet says he would go bankrupt if he saw all his clients as infrequently as he saw our dogs.

Family companion

The Stafford's character makes him extremely human friendly and he has a special affinity for children. In some countries he is known as the 'nanny dog'. He is intelligent and is fun to be with.

Whilst he is not very tall he is very strong; most people find that just looking at a Stafford gives them little idea of his strength. You really need to take a Stafford for a walk or generally handle him to fully appreciate his physical strength. Although he may love children, it is not advisable to let a young child exercise a Stafford unsupervised because of his strength.

Getting on with other dogs

The Staffordshire Bull Terrier was bred to be a fighting dog, and although the instincts that go with this have been hugely diluted, it is important to be aware of this part of his ancestry.

A Stafford will not naturally get on with other dogs unless he is socialized with dogs of sound temperament from an early age. If this is done, a Stafford will become tolerant of the dogs he meets, and he may even form close friendships with dogs he lives with. However, it is your job to work at socializing him to bring out the best in his character.

Living with other pets

Staffords will live with cats, rabbits and other small animals if introduced when they are young and if the introductions are carefully supervised. However, it is important to bear in mind that even though your Stafford likes your own cat, he may well take exception to the neighbor's cat if it strays into your garden.

Life expectancy

A Staffordshire Bull Terrier can live for 12 to 13 years, some longer, so caring for a Stafford is a big commitment. Of course, in return you will receive a great deal of love, many funny moments and a bucketful of anecdotes.

Staffords are never dull or boring companions and, providing you have some sense of humour, once you have been owned by one you will never wish to be without the breed.

Tracing back in time

The Stafford is a descendant of the old English Bulldog, who himself was descended from the mastiff-type dogs found across Europe, and often referred to, somewhat endearingly, as 'wide-mouthed' dogs. Unfortunately for them, these wide mouths were most commonly used for pugnacious and often bloody pastimes for the amusement of their owners.

The fighting breeds

The Bulldog was most famously used to bait bulls and to a lesser extent bears. There is written and pictorial evidence of these pastimes and the type of dogs used for them. In fact, the Bulldogs of this era bore little resemblance to the modern day Bulldog, as can be seen from the engraving, dated 1809

(opposite) titled Wasp, Child and Billy. The dogs are taller, lighter built animals with strong, broad heads and short muzzles.

When bull baiting lost its appeal – all these so-called 'sports' seemed to have peaks and troughs of popularity – the focus switched to the 'sport' of dog fighting. For this, a smaller, quicker dog was needed.

These were developed either from lighter Bulldogs or by mixing the Bulldog with a terrier of some kind – the most popular candidate being the now extinct English White Terrier. The new dogs became known as Bull and Terriers, and are featured in combat in The Westminster Pit, a print featured opposite.

Fighting undercover

The 1835 Cruelty to Animals Act made the UK the first country to ban dog fighting. However, under-cover fighting seems to have continued. Indeed, the spyhole depicted on the door on the right-handside of The Westminster Pit suggests that the spectators were being scrutinized. A further act was therefore passed in 1911- the Protection of Animals Act – to reinforce the dog fighting ban.

At this time, Bull and Terriers were kept in various parts of the UK, especially in mining areas or those where heavy industry flourished. Apart from being

Top Right:
Wasp, Child and Billy: Detail from a hand-colored engraving by H. G. Chalon, 1809.

Bottom Right:
The Westminster Pit, courtesy P & J Loughborough.

used in illegal fighting bouts, they were employed for badger baiting, ratting and such quirky 'sports' as fighting a monkey.

The legacy

The fact that this type of dog survived at all means that it must have had something special to offer to the general public. As they were predominantly owned by the lower orders, they would have lived cheek by jowl with their owners, so what was it that made them so attractive? Did the breed survive because of, or in spite of, its past history?

Firstly, it must be said that most dogs bite from fear. A dog descended from such gladiatorial stock could not afford to be afraid. Secondly, the aggression showed by Bull and Terriers was strictly confined to other dogs. According to the extant Rules and Agreements from the fighting days, at the end of each 'round' the dogs had to be separated by their human handlers and returned to their corners.

Looking at prints from this era, we can see that these handlers are completely unprotected – indeed, the sleeves of their shirts are rolled up, exposing their bare arms. Obviously they expect that the dogs will immediately differentiate between dog flesh and human contact.

There is also evidence that at the end of some fights, especially if the dog lost, he would be handed over to new owners. This made the Stafford a very adaptable type of dog.

In the right hands, a Stafford has an impeccable temperament.

Finally, to survive in the pit required quite a lot of 'on the spot' thinking if a dog was going to escape a damaging hold from his opponent. Staffords are interesting companions because they have an inherited ability to work things out and think for themselves.

It may surprise the modern reader to realize how much positive emphasis older breeders put upon the past history of the breed. I was brought up, as most of my generation of Stafford fanatics were, with the understanding that it is because of the breed's history that they are the reliable, human friendly dog that they undoubtedly are.

It seems that confusion has arisen in understanding the difference between a dog that is used for fighting another dog, and one that both fights and guards – in other words, where aggression, albeit controlled, may be directed towards humans as well as dogs. The Stafford has never been developed as a guard dog, and his temperament makes him unsuited to this role.

Facing page:
It is important to remember that, despite the Stafford's ancestry, aggression was never directed towards people.

Developing the breed

In the second half of the 19th century, dog shows began to be organized. The Bull Terrier was exhibited at shows as early as 1862. Bull Terrier breeders, especially those interested in the colored variety, used their Bull and Terrier cousins to a great extent to produce them. After some years the 'Stafford' was deemed to have done his job, and the Bull Terrier fraternity wished to separate the two breeds again.

It was as much to do with the Bull Terrier devotees as to the enthusiasm of the Stafford brotherhood that the Staffordshire Bull Terrier was recognized by the Kennel Club as a separate breed in 1935. The first Champions of the breed, Gentleman Jim and Lady Eve, gained their titles at Bath Championship Show in 1939.

In May 1935 a group of fanciers met in the Midlands at Cradley Heath to form a club, to be known as the Staffordshire Bull Terrier Club. It is important to note that there may have been many different types of 'fighting' dog around the UK, but it was the type most prevalent in the Black Country that became the foundation of the breed.

The Breed Standard

The next important task was to draw up a Breed Standard. The Standard of any breed is a blueprint of the ideal animal which breeders should aim to produce.

There was an immediate problem facing the fanciers who met to draw up this important document. The breed had lain fallow for so long, it was impossible to say that all the animals were 'pure' bred.

Bull Terrier blood had already been introduced, but who could tell if other breeds, especially those which may have shown themselves to be good working dogs, had not also been used? Certainly photographs of Bull Terriers and Staffordshire Bull Terriers of the 1930s show a much closer resemblance than examples of the two breeds do today.

The breed fanciers set about collecting records, photographs and sketches of Staffordshire

Bull Terrier bloodlines were used in the development of the Staffordshire Bull Terrier.

Bull Terriers, and they also called upon what is described as 'the lore and cumulative experience of generations'. They are also recorded as having two dogs, Jim the Dandy and Fearless Joe, present at the meeting.

In spite of the hotch potch that might have gone into producing Staffords over a number of years, they were able to identify features which occurred again and again, even among dogs which might vary in other respects. These features could be termed 'typical' for the breed and were therefore included in the Standard. So, evidently with some unanimity, a Description of the Breed was drawn up and this became the Standard as accepted by the Kennel Club.

Going global

The war years – 1939-1945 – curtailed the progress of the Staffordshire Bull Terrier in the show ring, but the breed was sufficiently well established to prosper once hostilities ceased. In 1935 registrations numbered only 147, but 13 years later they had reached 2,211 and the reputation of the breed was spreading overseas.

When Britons emigrated, they often took their dogs with them, and so the Stafford found new homes in Australia and South Africa, in particular, and later in the USA when it was recognized by the American Kennel Club in 1975.

What should a Stafford look like?

The original Breed Standard, drawn up in 1935, has had one or two alterations over the years but remains the blueprint for the breeders of today.

General appearance

The Stafford must show great strength for his comparatively small size, but at the same time he must look like an agile, active animal. He should also be 'balanced' – a doggy term which is hard to explain but in general means that all his parts should look as though they belong together. If you look at a Stafford – particularly where he stands among others of his own breed – and you think: 'what long legs he has' or conversely: 'how short and stubby he looks' then he is not balanced.

Characteristics and temperament

If you don't have the correct characteristics and temperament, you have lost the very essence of the Stafford – no matter how physically correct he might be.

As previously stated, the Stafford has inherited certain characteristics from his forebears. First is courage – and we must acknowledge what a positive attribute this is for any dog, especially in this fast and noisy modern age. Aggression can be taught and often stems from insecurity, but courage is 'bred in the bone' and is represented by a sensible, confident dog.

This is virtually the only Breed Standard that asks that the dog be friendly "especially with children", and there is certainly a bond between a Stafford and a child.

Head

The 1935 Breed Standard had a scale of points and in this no less than 30 of the 100 points was awarded to the head – which shows its importance. The head is a Stafford's most distinctive attribute – it marks him out as a Stafford and no other breed.

The head is broad but must be in balance with the rest of the body – a Stafford should not look like a tadpole. It must have strength, which means it is deep as well as broad, and that depth is particularly important in the foreface.

The ratio of the foreface to skull is roughly one-third foreface to two-thirds skull. These measurements are taken from the end of the nose to the stop (the step-up from the muzzle to the skull), and from the stop to the occiput bone at the base of the skull. These measurements are done in straight lines.

Looked at from above, the head tapers slightly to the nose, but this must only be gradual as a very pointed 'snipey' foreface is not desirable. The bone structure on the head is the basis for a lot of muscle development. Over the skull this musculature forms a line or furrow down the middle of the skull. At the side of the head there should be distinct muscles or 'cheek bumps'.

The stop is the pivot of the head. When a Stafford has the correct stop, the plane of his muzzle and that of his skull will almost be parallel. If the stop is too pronounced, the nose is higher than the stop and the dog is called 'dish faced' – the extreme of this is seen in the Boxer or the Bulldog.

If the stop is not properly defined then the head is termed 'down faced' – the extreme here being the Bull Terrier or the Borzoi.

The Stafford's head should be 'clean' – that is, there should be no loose flesh, sponginess around the muzzle, or wrinkle on the foreface.

Eyes

With so much Bull Terrier blood behind the Stafford, it is not unusual to see an almond-shaped eye, but this is not ideal and alters the expression of the animal, to its detriment. In breeds where the stop is extreme, the eye is bulbous (e.g. the Bulldog), but where the stop is shallow or non-existent, the eye is deep-set and triangular (e.g. the Bull Terrier). Where the Stafford has a correctly defined stop, his eye will be round and set to look straight ahead, neither deep-set nor bulbous. This gives the Stafford its essential look, which is bold but kind.

The eyes should be dark in color. There is a codicil that the color may 'bear some relation to coat color'. This is a sensible warning as a brown eye in a red dog may look perfect, whereas the same dark brown eye color in a black dog may look a little light.

The eyes are positioned at the front of the head which makes the Stafford very good at judging distances.

Ears

The ears of the Stafford should be set at the side of the head. Where the Bull Terrier influence has been strong, the ears tend to be placed high on the top of the skull with little space between. The best ear carriage is 'rose' although half prick is allowed. Full prick ears were allowable in the 1935 Standard, as, because of the Bull Terrier infusion, there were many prick-eared Staffords in the early days, but they are not permissible in today's Standard.

A rose ear has a crease which runs across the ear from its base, taking it in a backward direction. This then folds forward to the top edge of the ear. In a half-prick ear, the crease is not defined and the tip of the ear just turns over and forward.

Ears should be small and thin. Large heavy ears spoil the expression of the head. Good ears help a good head to look a super head. Unfortunately, the reverse can be said for poor ears – especially where they are large, thick and heavy.

Mouth

The lips in particular should be tight to the jaws and never hang down below the lower jaw. The jaws are big and strong and large enough to house large teeth. The teeth should be arranged in a perfect scissor bite, which means that the upper teeth closely overlap the lower teeth.

Neck

The Stafford is unlike most of the terrier breeds in that its Standard does not ask for a 'reach' of neck. In fact, quite the reverse, since the Standard says that the neck should be 'rather short'. This does not mean that there should be no length of neck but certainly eliminates a long, ewe-like reach of neck as is seen in some other terriers.

Below: The neck is short compared with other terrier breeds.

Forequarters

Unlike most breeds, the Stafford is shown face-on. This draws attention to his forequarters.

The front legs should be straight from the elbow to the pasterns. There is discernible muscle on the front legs and the bone should be substantial – but not flat or coarse.

The front should be wide. This sometimes causes problems for students of fighting breeds who see that many of these are narrow at the front.

The point is that the Bull and Terrier in the Black Country was distinguishable for being a shorter, wider dog than many others - his strength apparently being that it was hard to knock him off his feet.

The modern-day Stafford has kept this strong base and, in its turn, this base is dependant upon the way his shoulders are formed – to be precise, the angulation between the shoulder blade and the humerus or bone of the upper arm.

People try to impress with angle measuring, but it is usually best to use your eyes before you analyze what they are telling you. In simple terms, if you look at a breed like the Bulldog then his shoulders are so 'layed back' - i.e. the angle is so wide - that his body is virtually slung between his legs.

Conversely looking at a running dog, such as a Lurcher, the shoulders are so 'upright' that the front cannot be anything other than narrow.

The Stafford's front should lie between these two extremes. Where the shoulders are correct then the point of the elbows will go straight back – neither pointing inwards nor outwards.

The Staffordshire Bull Terrier's feet are of medium size, strong and well padded. One very typical characteristic of the Stafford, which is sometimes overlooked, is that the front feet should turn out a little and not point straight ahead or inwards.

In order for this to happen, there is a slight backwards slope from the foot to the wrist that allows the feet to turn out slightly. This should not be confused with weak pasterns where the whole foot looks flat.

With the correct lay-back and slight turn out the pastern is very springy and resilient – ideal for an active and agile dog.

Body

The body of the Stafford is best assessed from above and from the side. From above, you get a clear picture of his spring of rib; this should not be over-done, but yet he must not be flat or 'slab' sided. From behind the ribs, his waist should be nipped in before the swell of his well-muscled hindquarters. This definition of his body is a very characteristic attribute of a good Stafford.

The Stafford's ribcage is fairly long but his couplings – that is the unprotected part of his belly from the end of his last rib to the start of his hind legs – should be short. It is not desirable to breed for ultra short backs as this produces a less flexible animal – often such dogs have to swing their hind legs in order to move forward.

A level topline is an important element of the ideal Stafford. Some breeds have sway or a dip in their backs – this is not desirable in the Stafford. Alternatively others have a curved or 'roach' back – again, an undesirable trait in a Stafford. A fit Stafford will often have a crest of muscle over his hindquarters but he should never fall away over the hindquarters.

Interestingly, where a Stafford is too heavy, you are more likely to see a dip in his back whereas where

Facing page: The Stafford's body is well defined and muscular.

he is too lightly built you are most likely to see the roach or Whippet-like topline. This clause of the Standard also mentions width again, so there can be no doubting that throughout the ages men have looked for a rather wide front in a good Stafford.

Looking from the side is the way to see the length or shortness of a Stafford. But another thing you can check is the depth of his brisket. The ideal is where the brisket – or lowest edge of the ribs – ends just a tad below the elbow.

Where the brisket comes well below the elbow, the dog will appear too heavy and 'cloddy'. Where this point is above the elbow then the dog will appear to be too light and as if he is on stilts. This was not the original dog that was hard to knock off his feet!

Hindquarters

Many people comment upon the hindquarters of the Stafford – mainly because in a fit dog these are firmly muscled. In fact, the firmness or even hardness to the touch of a Stafford in fit condition is something that breeders are proud of.

The hindquarters are the Stafford's powerhouse. He drives himself forwards on the move and, in play, these are the pistons that allow jumping to amazing heights.

The stifles should be well bent and where this occurs the hock will turn down towards the ground. There is therefore a nice curve to the dog's hind legs. If the stifle is not bent then his legs appear to be in a straight line, and the hocks are forced to point up in the air. It is also quite common to see the reverse, where the hind legs are over-angulated. Here, the hind legs of the dog will stretch out behind him with the hocks well beyond the pelvis.

Such a dog is at a disadvantage in the running and jumping stakes as he will have to 'collect his legs' before he can propel himself forward. A correctly built Stafford is like a coiled spring and can snap into action instantly.

Looking from behind the dog, his legs must be parallel. If his hocks turn in towards each other he is called 'cow hocked', and if the hocks turn out he is called 'pin toed' as the toes are forced inwards towards one another.

Feet

A lot of attention should be paid to a Stafford's feet. At the front they should be halfway between the cat and the hare in size. The small, neat cat foot, well knuckled up, is attractive superficially but a larger, clumpier foot is more able to grip the ground in a tussle. The hare foot is usually associated with poor bone and splayed toes. Very often such a foot – with its long toes – does not sufficiently rub against the floor and causes problems for the owners when nails become too long.

With the clumpier foot come thick pads – another desirable feature, giving him stability. The nails should be black, unless there is white on the toes in which case they may be pink. A well-constructed foot should rarely, if ever, need its nails cut once the dog is out of puppyhood.

Tail

Most of the Stafford Standard is couched in pretty down to earth terms. However, when they got to the tail the fanciers suddenly waxed lyrical with talk such as 'should not curl much and may be likened to an old-fashioned pump handle'. It is a thin, tapering tail, and in the UK, it is common to accentuate this in the show ring by trimming the hairs off the tail.

The ideal length is generally accepted as reaching – when held straight – to the hock or just below, and it is quite thick at the base. The tail must be set low, which means that the tail emerges from the hip bones, covers the anus and slopes down in a gentle curve. It must be said that a tail set too high does spoil the balance of the dog.

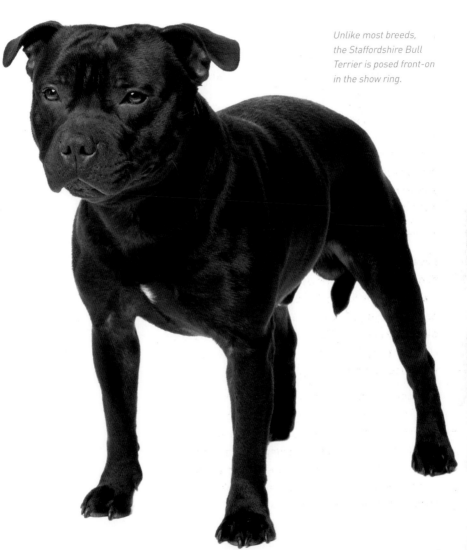

Unlike most breeds, the Staffordshire Bull Terrier is posed front-on in the show ring.

Movement

A movement clause was only included in the Staffordshire Bull Terrier Standard in 1987 – quite surprising when you consider that this is an 'active and agile dog' according to part one of the Standard.

The keynote for the correct movement of a Stafford is that it is free and purposeful. At the front he should lift his front legs only slightly off the ground – that is with an economy of movement. It might look pretty if he prances or moves like a hackney horse but it is not typical. We could hear the click, click of the front feet on one of our best moving dogs every time he crossed the kitchen floor.

The rear is where the real action takes place, and this is why he needs his muscles. The rear legs go straight into the tracks of the front. Providing that he is well constructed, you will virtually see a tunnel between his front and rear legs when he walks away from or towards you. If he is cow hocked or pin toed then his rear legs will mask his front. If his shoulder placement is wrong then he may well approach you with forelegs crossing or elbows pointing outwards. Good handlers in the show ring can hide many faults or failings in their charges when standing, but once on the move the dog is on his own!

Movement should be
free and purposeful.

It is in the movement phase that the Stafford is seen to be very different from the average terrier. He moves with such forcefulness and power from the rear. He drives himself forwards rather than daintily springing up and down along the ground. The Stafford also has a happy knack of moving at two different speeds – and if you don't get the proper speed for him he may well start to roll rather than drive along. So, if you intend to show your dog, do practice the speed at which you walk him until you are sure that you are getting the right speed for him to really show his paces!

Coat

The Stafford's coat is short; the hairs lie close to his skin and if he is in good condition it will shine like satin. It should fit closely and not have any wrinkles or folds so that it shows off all his muscle and accentuates the definition of his body.

Color

We are so lucky in Staffords that we have such a variety of colors. The basic colors are tan and black with their dilute forms fawn and blue. Brindle is a pattern and so we have a wide variety of very pretty brindle colors from silver to mahogany, depending on the arrangement of the tan to the black hairs.

Blue was not mentioned as a color for Staffords in the 1935 Standard. They are now very common as pets, but not so often seen in the ring as the coloration is often accompanied by an undesirable feature, such as a slate-grey nose or yellow eye.

All-white Staffords, as all-black Staffords, are rarely seen but they do crop up now and again. Red or brindle pied – that is predominantly white dogs with some brindle or red (tan) patches – are popular. The tan colorings vary from deep red to the dilute pale fawn.

Liver – a very deep red color – which is often accompanied by green eyes and brown noses, is considered a fault, as is the black-and-tan color in a Stafford. Red Staffords with white chests and black masks are permissible. But a Stafford should not be tri-colored, i.e. red, black and white coloring throughout.

Also be wary of acquiring a so-called merle Stafford. This is not a color that occurs naturally in the breed and so these dogs cannot be registered.

Height and Weight

Much has been written about the Stafford's height and weight, chiefly because in the revised 1948 Standard the height was lowered from a range of

16-18 inches (40.5-45.7 cm) down to 14-16 inches (35.5-40.5 cm). In fact, this did not mean that half the Stafford population were debarred from the show ring as most were around the 16 inch (40.5 cm) mark anyway. One of the shortest Stafford Champions of all time, Ch. Head Lad of Vilmar, advertised at 14 inches (36.8 cm) and did his winning long before the change in the Standard. The change came to keep the Standard in tune with the dog as it existed.

As time has progressed many of us have reason to bless the reduction. Anyone wanting a guard dog will look for an animal taller than 16 inches, and that suits us fine as the Stafford is not a natural guard anyway. All these measurements are taken from the ground to the withers i.e the highest point of the shoulders.

As for the weight, the Standard states: dogs 13-17kg (28-38lb); bitches 11-15.4 kg (24-34 lb).

Summing up

The Staffordshire Bull Terrier has survived many vicissitudes since it was recognized in 1935. The breed has maintained its own particular character and its physical appearance has altered very little. The Stafford is still an easy maintenance, healthy, natural, no-nonsense sort of dog. Long may he continue to give us pleasure and affection.

What do you want from a Stafford?

When my husband and I kept a boarding kennel, we were amazed at the number of people who had quite simply chosen the wrong type of dog for their lifestyle.

The lady who hated grooming yet had chosen a Tibetan Terrier, the couple who disliked walking but had bought a Pointer, the flat dweller who selected a Border Collie – bred on a farm to boot. Rescue kennels are full of the fall-out from such mistakes. It is essential to study the various breeds before making a final choice. The Stafford is a very versatile breed but even we have to admit that it is not the ideal companion for everyone or every circumstance.

Companionship

The Stafford is a dog which needs human companionship. A Stafford's true character is never fully developed unless he is a member of a family, and he will pine if he is relegated to a kennel environment. If you are away from home for lengthy periods every day, a Stafford is not the breed for you. If you have children in the family, you can make no better choice. The Stafford is an enthusiastic playmate, and a loyal, loving companion.

Trainability

I was recently contacted by a new owner who said he was having trouble with training his young Stafford. "All I want is a calm, submissive dog," he said. I could only tell him that he had chosen the wrong breed. If you want a dog who will sit quietly in his bed and ignore your visitors then this is not the dog for you. However, the Stafford is a highly intelligent dog, and if you 'think Stafford', and put in some time and effort, you will have a well-behaved companion, who understands his place in the family pack. If you want to get involved in one of the canine sports, such as agility or flyball, a Stafford will be an enthusiastic competitor.

Guard dog

A common misconception among people buying
a Stafford is the belief that they will prove to be
good guards. They were never developed as guards
and many finish in rescue because they have
disappointed their owners in this respect. They have
a natural instinct to protect a child, or a weaker
member of the family, but that is a far as it goes.
A Stafford should be celebrated for his friendly,
outgoing personality, and should never be acquired
by those wanting a macho companion to
boost their own self-esteem.

*Right: If you are looking
for a guard dog, choose
another breed.*

What does your Stafford want from you?

The top priority is to choose a dog that suits your lifestyle, but make sure that you also think of what a dog needs from you. The Staffordshire Bull Terrier is a low-maintenance dog in terms of his daily care, but like all breeds, he has his own special needs which you must be aware of.

Giving time

The early months of a Stafford's life require almost total commitment from yourself. These are the months when you will teach your Stafford most of

the lessons he will need for life, and the more effort you put into these months the better reward you will receive in later years. When your Stafford becomes an adult, make sure he is included in activities and feels an integral member of the family. A Stafford should never be left on his own for long periods; he will be thoroughly miserable and may become destructive.

Exercise requirements

Staffords do not need miles and miles of exercise – although if you have the time and the inclination they will definitely appreciate it. A dog such as a Border Collie, especially one from farm stock, really must have miles of free running. A Stafford can be very happy with a short walk and a quarter of an hour chasing a ball – violent exercise is what suits him best. A Stafford will also take to road walking, which helps to keep his nails short, and while he is young gives him experience of the outside world.

Promoting the Stafford

Anyone who has ever spent time with a Stafford will be aware of the breed's excellent temperament and character. The Stafford is highly intelligent, inquisitive to the point of nosiness, versatile, courageous and enthusiastic about everything apart from a visit to the vet and – his most endearing quality – he possesses innate friendliness towards humans. Unfortunately, if mismanaged, these positive attributes can become negatives.

More than ever before, Staffords need to be given opportunities to rise above the purpose for which they were originally bred while retaining both the positive characteristics of that inheritance and their versatility. As a Stafford owner, you need to plan a program of socialization so that your dog can cope with a wide range if situations, without feeling worried or threatened.

It is particularly important that he is socialized with other dogs. The Stafford's specific function as a fighting dog has become obsolete but negative association lives on and we must continue to concentrate on developing the image of the breed so that the Stafford is viewed by others as we view him ourselves.

Right: Responsible Stafford owners should seek to promote the breed in the best possible light.

Extra considerations

Before you start looking for a Staffordshire Bull Terrier, you need to make a few more decisions to narrow your choice.

Male or female?

If you are sure you have enough energy, forbearance and sense of humour to take on a Stafford, then your next choice must be which sex.

The male of any breed, with his high testosterone level, is more inclined to be dominant, especially in any tussle with another dog. On the other hand, if trained properly, a male makes the more interesting, and often the more loyal, companion.

Stafford bitches can also fall out with other dogs, although not so violently or frequently. They are usually more 'self centred' than males. Perhaps because they would be the ones to raise the next generation, they tend to have a better idea of what is 'best' for them.

A female Stafford will play with a ball just as long as it interests her, and will then walk away to find a better amusement. They are often more greedy than the males.

Bitches will have twice-yearly 'season' or 'heats' which can cause problems if there are many dogs in your area and especially if these are allowed to roam.

Most vets will spay bitches before their first season – there are some medical advantages to this, such as a reduced risk of mammary tumors.

It is not necessary for a bitch to have a litter. This will not 'fulfil' her – that is giving dogs human feelings. Nor would I advise using a dog at stud unless you are able to offer him a steady supply of bitches, which will involve showing him successfully.

In general, dogs not used at stud will settle down after 'puberty' and will not hanker after what they have not known. Conversely, once used at stud he will be more likely to look for, and run after, another bitch.

More than one?

It is not a good idea to buy two puppies from the same litter or indeed to have two Staffords who are close in age. Training, socializing and general bonding is much harder to achieve. The one-to-one relationship between a Stafford and his owner is the ideal.

If you already have another dog in the family, then it may be best to select the opposite sex for your new puppy.

In general it will be easy to introduce a bitch puppy to another bitch or to an adult dog, but it is definitely not a good idea to try to run two male animals together – unless there is a great difference in age. The male dominance issue will raise its head one day and many Staffords end up in rescue as a result of their owners having two male Staffords in the one family.

Socializing with other dogs outside the family at an early age is essential. But always make sure that the dogs he meets are friendly. A Stafford can remember if he is beaten up when young and will be on his toes to get his revenge when he is older – a revenge on all dogs, or maybe just the ones that remind him of his original aggressor.

An older dog?

Having a puppy in the house is hard work, and some people prefer to take on an older, fully trained dog. There are advantages in getting a mature dog, apart from the hope that he is house trained and finished with chewing.

The character of the dog is now obvious. So if you love walking and the outdoor life, a very lively, active Stafford could be for you. On the other hand if you are more housebound, a quiet older Stafford could be just the thing.

Facing page: It may suit your lifestyle to take on an older dog.

There are a number of excellent breed rescue groups as well as the more well known national animal rescue organizations to help you. Workers from the rescue group will want to check your home conditions and your attitude to the breed. In turn, they should be able to give you some idea of the history of the dog on offer or alternatively have a fair idea of his character if he has been assessed in one of their kennels. You will be required to neuter your new charge.

Any dog needs a great deal of time and a lot of commitment. The lessons he learns in the first few months of his life will affect him for the rest of his mature years. At times you may begin to think that he will 'never learn this lesson' but perseverance on your part will pay off when you find you own a well adjusted, happy dog that is a pleasure to live with.

Of course, if you take an older dog who has some problems then you have to put extra time into his re-training. Often the rescue group will be able to give you expert advice.

Health issues

The Staffordshire Bull Terrier is a remarkably healthy breed but there are a few hereditary diseases which can be passed from generation to generation. Breeding stock can be health tested for some of these.

The Stafford has three main problems:

- A brain condition L2Hydroxyglutaric aciduria (L-2-HGA) for which there is a DNA test.

- Hereditary Juvenile Cataracts (HC) for which there is also a DNA test.

- Persistent Hyperplastic Primary Vitreous (PHPV) for which, unfortunately there is no DNA test at present. However, there is a test for its presence in a dog, and this examination can be performed on a puppy from six weeks of age.

For further information on hereditary conditions, see page 182.

For further information on hereditary conditions, see page 182.

Below: It is important to check that the breeder has carried out essential health checks.

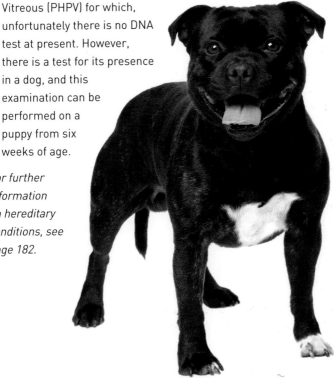

Sourcing a puppy

Having decided that you really would like a Stafford and that you have a Stafford-friendly home, the next most important question is where to source it from. Never has that consideration been more important than it is today.

There are many different 'types' of Staffordshire Bull Terriers advertised in many outlets from the internet to newspapers. It must therefore be stressed that there is only one recognized breed of Staffordshire Bull Terrier, and the best way for you to track down a litter is to contact your local Staffordshire Bull Terrier Breed Club. The secretary will have details of breeders in your area, and they may know of upcoming litters. Contact details can be found on national Kennel Club websites.

The term 'breeder' covers such a wide spectrum – from the pet owner who decides to have one litter from their bitch up to the person who has been

breeding for the show ring for many years and over many generations. In between are those who have a little knowledge but not a great deal of experience, and those who have a lot of experience in producing numerous litters, but who are only interested in breeding as an extra form of income.

If you contact the secretary of a breed club, it should maximise your chances of finding a 'proper' and caring breeder. Even so, I advise you to approach the selection of your puppy with you head and not your heart.

Questions to ask

Find out as much as you can about the litter before you go and see them. Puppies are irresistible, and it is very hard to make an objective decision when you are surrounded by a litter of Stafford pups who all seem to be saying: "take me home!" The questions you should ask include the following:

- How many are in the litter?

- What is the split of males and females?

- What colors are they?

- Have they been reared in the home rather than in an outside kennel?

- Have they been socialized with a variety of different people and got used to the comings and goings of family life?

- Will I be able to see the mother with her puppies?

- Is there any evidence of inherited disorders in the bloodlines? Have the parents been health checked?

If you want to get involved in showing, you will also need to find out more information about the bloodlines that have been used, and whether there are any puppies of show quality in the litter.

Questions to answer

A good, reputable breeder will want to find out as much as he can about you to ensure you can provide a suitable home for a Stafford. If the only thought is 'have you got the money?' then that breeder is best left alone.

The questions you may be asked include the following:

- Have you owned dogs/Staffordshire Bull Terriers before?

- What is your family set up? The breeder will want to know whether you have children and what age they are, whether you have anyone else, such as an elderly or frail relative, living with you?

- Is the dog likely to be left on his own during the day – if, so, for how long?

- Do you have a secure garden?

- Are you interested in showing your Stafford?

If you are happy with the answers you have received, and the breeder is confident that you can provide a good home for a Stafford, you can make an appointment to go and see the puppies.

Puppy watching

Ideally, you will be able to see the puppies when they are around six weeks of age. By this stage, they will be actively exploring their surroundings, and interacting with each other and with people.

The litter should have been reared in the house, which will give them the maximum amount of socialization with people and with household noises, such as washing machines and vacuum cleaners. The living quarters should be as clean as possible. Puppies make a mess, but there should be adequate facilities for disinfecting their quarters. Puppies who are allowed or left to wallow in their own dirt often grow into dirty adults.

Signs of a healthy litter

The puppies should look healthy. They should have shiny coats, be full of life and not have swollen tummies. Distended tummies are a sign of worms (see page 162). A good breeder will give you details as to when and how the puppies were wormed.

Make sure that you see the mother and that she is of a sound and happy temperament. A Stafford mother may well be very defensive of her puppies while their eyes are closed – that is before 10 days old. As a result, a caring breeder will not want you to visit at this time. Once the puppies have opened their eyes and are beginning to explore, the mother should be happy for you to look at her puppies.

The father may not be present on the premises. Most breeders will need to travel in order to find the right mate for their bitch. Only occasionally will a breeder be lucky enough to own a dog that absolutely suits their bitch.

I would be wary if I found that a breeder had a number of bitches, all mated to his own dog, and that dog had little or no recognition in the show ring. My suspicion would be that this is a breeder who is churning out puppies for the money.

*Facing page:
It is important to see
the mother with
her puppies.*

You should expect the puppies to come straight out to greet you, wagging their tails. Do not be tempted to fall in love with the one who hides in the corner. Properly reared Stafford puppies are confident and out-going. Also be wary of one that is considerably smaller than his littermates. He may be just a late developer, but may also have some underlying problem. Time will tell which of these scenarios is correct, but it should be the responsibility of the breeder to keep this type of puppy long enough to see how he turns out.

Show Puppy

If you are selecting a puppy with the hope of exhibiting him at shows, you will need to be even more careful with your research

Read as much as you can on the breed, and include at least one book which has a detailed analysis of the Breed Standard. But no matter how well you have prepared yourself, it is advisable to view puppies with a friend who has some knowledge of the finer points of the breed.

Look for a puppy with good bone, squarely built, with a rather wide front and a body that feels quite chunky when you pick him up. Most important of all, make sure that the puppy has a promising head – that is that he has round eyes, set wide apart, and his ears are set on the side and not at the top of his head. His foreface at this stage should be quite blunt – a pointed nose at this age will just get more and more pointed as puppy grows. A head never gets any better than it is at eight weeks old – too often, the head gets weaker.

Do not be carried away by too much salesmanship – especially if it includes promises of a glowing show career. Many Staffords are born every year, but only a very few reach Champion status.

Getting
ready

Before you bring a puppy into your home, try to spend a little time thinking about how you want to integrate him into the family – it will pay dividends in the long run.

It is easier to teach a puppy to conform to the house rules you set down than to break bad habits in a youngster who has been allowed to run amok. It is a good idea to have a family conference and lay down the house rules before you collect your puppy.

House rules

The first thing that should be decided is where the pup should sleep. Although the Stafford is a strong, 'tough' breed he is particularly susceptible to the cold.

Muscle and bone he may have, but he is very short on the protective coat front. Unlike many dogs, a Stafford has no length or density of coat and, unlike many

terrier breeds, he does not have a 'double' coat. It follows that you should find a warm and draught-free spot for your Stafford's bed.

You must also decide if you want your Stafford to share your furniture. It is tempting to put a little pup beside you on the settee, but will he be as welcome when he is fully grown? Some people give the dog his 'own' chair, or they are happy to let him share with them, perhaps an extra throw will come in handy to protect the upholstery?

Whatever you decide, start as you mean to go on – changing this rule can cause confusion in the dog's mind. From the start make sure that he knows that even if it is 'his' chair, he must come off it if you ask him to.

There may be parts of the house you wish to keep dog free. It must be said that the more freedom a Stafford can enjoy around the house, the more relaxed and well adjusted he will become. But this is not to say that you should not have boundaries. If you don't want him to go upstairs for example, buy a baby gate to prevent access to 'no go' areas.

In the garden

The greatest concern here is safety. Ponds, streams and rivers hold a fatal attraction for dogs; Stafford puppies will not be afraid to let their curiosity get the better of them and take a dip.

Below: Try to see your home from a puppy's perspective.

I would not attempt to keep a Stafford in anything other than an enclosed garden. Even then, the enclosure must be secure. Take a slow tour round the perimeter of your garden and check the fencing or the hedge if that marks the boundary. A Stafford can squeeze through the smallest gap and through the thickest hedges – he is not even put off by thorns, although he may be very dejected afterwards if he is pierced!

Make sure that you cover any holes. If you have a fence, it must be high and robust. I had a friend whose Stafford was unable to scale his tall fence, so he simply bulldozed his way through!

You will need a secure gate, preferably bolted from the inside. The danger is not only that your Stafford might wander out and get run over, but unfortunately Staffords are a target for dog thieves. They make themselves easy targets because they are so friendly and trusting, even of strangers.

Finding a vet

Before your puppy arrives home, you should find and register yourself with a vet. Visit some of the vets in your local area, and speak to other pet owners you might know, to see who they use or who they recommend. Word of mouth is really the best recommendation.

When you contact a veterinary practice, find out the following:

- Does the surgery run an appointment system?

- What are the arrangements for emergency, out of hours cover?

- Do any of the vets in the practice have experience treating Staffies?

- What facilities are available at the practice?

Also find out about the regime for inoculations. When you make your first visit with the puppy you can ask your vet's advice about setting up a worming regime.

Facing page: The Stafford can squeeze through the smallest gap and hurdle a high fence, so make sure your garden is secure.

Buying Equipment

Before your pup arrives, you will need to decide what equipment to buy.

Dog Bed

A young Stafford is best suited to having a plastic bed lined with synthetic fleece type blankets. Pretty duvets and soft foam beds may be all right for the older dog, but are far too vulnerable for the teeth of a young, growing Stafford.

Some people like to train their pup from the first to sleep in a cage or crate – even if this is with the door open. A Stafford that is used to such a set up can be easily taken to stay in a stranger's house or a hotel, and will be content to stay in his crate if a visitor comes to the house who is afraid or allergic to dogs. The spaces between the wires of the cage or crate must be smaller than the width of the puppy's jaws, as there is a danger when he is very young of his teeth becoming stuck. A crate for an adult Stafford should be at least 2ft x 2ft x 3ft 6in (60cm x 60cm x 105cm).

Bowls

As well as his bed, your Stafford will need a feeding bowl and a water bowl. Never use your own china for a dog. Stainless steel bowls are the safest to buy – other types may look pretty but they are easily chewed or broken. A pup or an older dog could take it into his head to have a game with his bowl and throw it around, which could prove dangerous if the bowl is breakable.

Below: A Stafford puppy will soon learn to settle.

Food

The breeder should provide you with a diet sheet, and if you can ask for it in advance of getting your puppy you will be able to buy the necessary supplies in readiness.

Collar and Lead

A narrow collar and a lightweight lead are suitable for a young puppy. You can let the puppy wear his collar around the house before taking him out for walks, but do this under supervision as he will try to scratch and get the collar off if he can.

When fitting the collar, you should be able to get your fingers between the collar and the neck. If it is any tighter it will cause discomfort; if it is any looser the puppy could pull backwards out of the collar and run away. As a puppy grows and his neck thickens, you will need to buy larger-size collars.

When choosing a lead for a Stafford opt for leather rather than chain. It may be a nuisance if your Stafford starts to chew his lead – but train him, with firmness and kindness, not to do this. The half leather/half chain leads are terribly hard on your hands and prevent you using the lead properly

Some dogs do better in a harness – especially if they are bad pullers on the lead – but choose a plain nylon harness not the decorated 'fighting' dog type. Harnesses which are decorated with metal badges or shields are emblematic of the fighting dog and therefore give out the wrong impression.

Wait until your Stafford is fully grown before buying an expensive leather collar.

ID

Your Stafford needs to wear some form of ID when he is out in public places. This can be in form of a disc, engraved with your contact details, that can be attached to the collar. When your Stafford is older, you can buy an embroidered collar with your contact details, which eliminates the danger of the disc becoming detached from the collar.

You may also wish to consider a permanent form of ID. Increasingly breeders are getting puppies' micro chipped before they go to their new homes. But if your puppy has not been micro chipped, you can ask your vet to do it, maybe when he goes along for his vaccinations.

Toys

Most people like to buy toys for their dogs. Balls, frisbees and anything that can be thrown and chased after are very popular with Staffords. He might think that a stick is the best thing of all, but these can be highly dangerous and every year vets see dogs badly injured when, for example, the sharp end of a stick pierces the roof of a dog's mouth.

The key thing with toys for a Stafford is safety. A Stafford can so easily destroy plastic or rubber toys, and small chewed off pieces, or squeaks, can cause lots of problems.

The best choice is a really strong, hard rubber ball or a kong. Staffords also like tug toys, but again you must make sure that the tug toy is made of robust material. If you intend to show your pup, it is best to leave pulling toys until he is older as it takes many months for the teeth to be fully set in a dog's gums.

Grooming equipment

All Stafford coats benefit from an occasional stiff brush, followed by a rub down with a soft, possibly velvet cloth or grooming glove. A good pair of nail clippers may prove useful and certainly a tooth brush and paste will help keep your pet's teeth in good order.

Below: The toys you buy must be suitably robust.

Settling in

When you go to fetch your pup, take a blanket and some newspaper with you. He may well be sick on the journey home as it will, most probably, be the first time that he has been in a car.

On arriving home, let him explore at his own pace – everything is strange and new to him and it will take him a little time to get his bearings. Take him outside and stay with him. Speak to him all the time to encourage him and to make the sound of your voice familiar to him.

Meeting the family

If you have children, try to keep them as calm as possible – not an easy task when faced with such an exciting thing as a new puppy. But you can explain to the children the importance of not letting the pup get over excited, plus the dangers of hurting him if they rush around too much. Most dangerous of all is allowing a child to pick up the puppy. Stafford puppies are strong and can easily wriggle free.

A fall from any height can cause considerable damage – even broken limbs. So make sure the child is sitting on the floor before being allowed to hold the pup.

Even a dog as steady as a Stafford needs a break from play sometimes and puppies, especially, need plenty of time for sleep. Children should therefore be taught right from the outset that when the pup or dog is in his bed, he should be left alone.

The Animal Family

If you already have a pet or pets in your home, you will need to plan how you are going to introduce the newcomer.

If you have another dog, it is probably best to make the introduction in the garden. This will be viewed as neutral ground where the puppy cannot immediately take over the resident dog's territory. If the adult dog has toys he particularly loves, it would be best to put them away until you are sure that the two are on good terms.

Speak to the older animal and reassure him that the pup is something to be accepted by all the family. The resident animal may feel that he is being set aside for the newcomer so remember to give him plenty of pats and lots of talk, even though the

endearing youngster is striving to attract all the attention. Be particularly careful at feeding time and when giving any treats. All interactions with food should be fully supervised.

If you have a cat, make sure he has places where he can get out of the puppy's way, preferably a higher surface he can escape to.

Don't let the puppy tease the cat or he may get a nasty scratch. A simple box round the ears from the cat to warn pup off is a necessary lesson, but if pushed too far, the cat might really scratch. If he hits pup's eyes then a really serious injury could result. In time, the pair will learn to live together in harmony – and they may even become good friends.

Small animals such as rabbits, hamsters and birds could be more problematic. It is, after all, natural for a dog to chase a rabbit for food! The best plan is to allow the pup to see the rabbit, hamster or bird while it is in the safety of its hutch or cage, and just observe his reactions.

Take things step by step – let the puppy look, sniff, and explore over a number of days so that they are really familiar with each other. In time, the novelty will wear off and most Staffords will lose interest. However, it is better to be safe than sorry, so make sure your Stafford is never left unsupervised in the vicinity of small, caged animals.

Mealtimes

You should have received a diet sheet from the breeder. It is really important that you stick to this as far as you possibly can at least for the first few days. A sudden change in diet could upset his tummy which will make settling in even more stressful for him.

For information on choosing a diet, see page 102.

For information on choosing a diet, see page 102.

Below: To begin with your puppy will need four meals a day.

The first night

The first night that pup is at home with you can be quite traumatic. Litters of puppies always snuggle up together – often in a great ball with everyone fighting to get on the lowest level and thus be covered by warm littermates.

For the first night, or even first few nights, the pup will definitely miss his siblings. It is therefore very important that he has a warm, cosy bed. You can also put a hot-water bottle (preferably, if you can get one, a stone type) wrapped tightly in a blanket and not too hot, and place it in the bed.

Some people put a ticking clock wrapped in a towel beside pup – the idea being that the tick of the clock will sound like the beat of its littermates' hearts.

The one 'cure' that you should never try – although it has a 100 per cent success rate – is to take pup to bed with you. No breed appreciates a warm bed more than a Stafford. For the sake of avoiding a couple of disturbed nights, you could have a life time of bed sharing. An eight-week-old pup is easily accommodated, but a fully grown Stafford is not.

Facing page:
It is inevitable that
your puppy will miss
the company of his
littermates to
begin with.

House training

The most important lesson your puppy now has to learn is house training. Nothing is worse than a dirty dog. Staffords in general are clean animals, and your puppy should learn quite quickly to perform outside.

Dogs are creatures of habit, and if you establish a routine of taking your puppy outside at regular intervals, he will soon learn what is required.

The times to take a puppy out are:

- First thing in the morning

- Last thing at night

- After every meal

- When he wakes from a nap

- After a play session.

A puppy will need to relieve himself every two hours; he will learn to be clean more quickly if you can manage to take him out every hour.

The best plan is to allocate an area of the garden for toileting, and take your puppy to this spot every time. Use a special word, such as "Busy", and, in time, he will learn to perform on command. This is most useful when you are traveling and have only a few comfort stops – usually, of course, determined by the human family! Remember to be lavish with praise when your Stafford co-operates.

At first, the pup may not be able to hold his water all night. So make some allowance for this. If you have a crate, you can line the front of it with a newspaper, so your puppy does not have to soil his bedding.

When accidents happen

It is inevitable that your puppy will have the odd accident – and this will usually be your fault. You may not have spotted the tell-tale signs that he is about to relieve himself – sniffing and circling – or you may have left it too long between trips out to the garden.

Therefore you should never scold your puppy for making a mistake. If you catch him in the act simply pick him up and take him to his toiling area.

Hopefully, he will finish his business out there, and you can then praise him for going in the right place. If you discover a mess in the house, do not attempt to reprimand your puppy – he will have no idea what you are angry about. All you can do is clean it up, using a pet deodorizer so he is not tempted to use that spot again, and make sure you are more vigilant in the future.

Choosing a diet

The most important consideration as far as daily care is concerned is how you are going to feed your Staffordshire Bull Terrier. Convenience may be taken into account, but more important is to choose a diet which best suits your dog – and his requirements may well change over his lifetime.

Natural diet

You may choose to feed a fully natural diet such as the BARF (Biologically Appropriate Raw Food) diet, which involves giving raw meat and bones. This is just as if the dog had killed an animal and eaten the whole thing – which in the wild is what he would do.

Alternatively you could buy meat from the butcher or dog meat, often sold in sausage form. To this you should add dog meal or biscuit. Feeding this type of food you must be sure that you are giving the dog all the minerals, carbohydrates and proteins that he needs.

Commerical diets

A ready-made commercial food can be either canned meat, plus biscuit, or a complete diet. Complete foods are extremely easy and clean to serve, but they are very high in protein so should be given in the exact amounts recommended by the manufacturers.

Whenever you feed a commercial food – and there are dozens on the market – be wary of making additions. Commercial food producers have invested heavily in research in order to give the correct balance of ingredients. Additions may upset this balance and could cause problems for your dog.

In extreme cases deformation of the limbs has occurred in dogs that have been fed too many additives.

Feeding regime

When your Stafford puppy first arrives home, he will need four meals a day. It will be to your advantage later in his life if you have not skimped on giving him top-quality food.

As your pup develops, he may well start to refuse or pick at one of his meals. This may be around the 10 to 11 week stage. After about 10 months he will probably be down to two meals, and after 18 months – the age where he will have completed most, although not all, of his growing – he could go down to one meal a day. A Stafford is not fully mature, physically or mentally, until he is about four years of age.

A young puppy should have a good covering and feel quite chunky to the touch – there is time enough to harden him up when he is older. So don't be mean with the amount of food you are giving at this stage.

Bones and chews

Giving bones is a subject open for discussion. Most vets will tell you never to give them – they see problems from bones stuck in gullets or severe constipation due to the dog having too many bones.

But there is nothing a dog enjoys more than a big knuckle-bone. If you are going to give bones they must be big and raw to prevent splintering.

There are many types of chews now on the market – from narrow strips through to large pig's ears, and some that clean the dog's teeth. These products are very popular but must be used by the Stafford owner with some care. In no time at all the Stafford can reduce a chew to a mush which they sometimes try to swallow with awful results.

Ideal Weight

The key to feeding an adult Stafford is to balance the amount of food with the amount of exercise he gets. In recent years in the show ring it has become increasingly popular to go for the 'stripped out look' in Staffords. This follows the fashionable look among our young women – the search for that magic size zero. Now if this look in a Stafford is obtained by giving the correct amount of food together with a lot of vigorous exercise, then all well and good, but too often it seems that this is achieved by restricting the intake of food. The tell-tale signs of this regime is a dull coat and a drawn look to the dog. A significant side effect of reducing the weight of a Stafford is that you tend to make him more active. Taken to extremes, the dog can become far too hyped up for comfortable living. In such cases it is surprising how quickly an increase in weight can calm the dog down.

The other end of the spectrum is the problem of too much weight. This is rarely seen in the show ring, but is far too often evident in the world of pet dogs. The obese dog is ugly, and prone to injuries and other health problems. There is no doubt that carrying too much weight can shorten a dog's life. So don't let your Stafford become a couch potato in your efforts to get away from the coiled spring scenario – there is a happy medium.

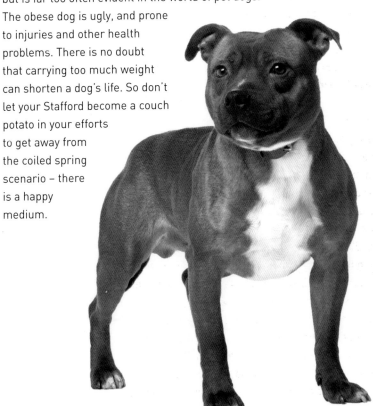

Caring for your Stafford

The Staffordshire Bull Terrier is a hardy, low-maintenance breed, but you are responsible for all his needs, so you should adopt a regime of daily care.

Grooming

In terms of coat care, the Staffordshire Bull Terrier must be one of the easiest breeds to care for. His short smooth coat lies close to the skin, and when a dog is in good health it positively gleams.

He does not need extensive grooming to keep his coat in good order. A simple going over with a stiff brush will quickly rid him of dirt or loose hairs.

Although the Stafford is a tough dog, he has almost no hair on his tummy, and therefore this part of his anatomy should be dried after walks in the wet.

His feet will not come to any harm if left wet and muddy – but your kitchen floor will suffer!

It is a good idea to accustom your Stafford to being groomed from an early age, and then he will learn to enjoy the procedure. Make sure you have some treats at the ready and reward him when he is calm and still. In time, he will relax and enjoy being groomed. Make a point of brushing through the coat on a weekly basis.

Show dogs get extra attention before they are exhibited in the ring but, compared to most breeds, this is pretty straightforward. An exhibitor may trim a Stafford's tail to neaten its appearance and give the correct 'pump-handle' look. This is done by scissoring the underside of the tail. In addition, the coat will be 'polished' with a chamois leather to bring out the shine.

Bathing

Your dog may need a bath from time to time. Most Staffords are quite fond of rolling in awful things that can smell overpowering! Make sure you use dog shampoo or baby shampoo, and soap him with care, making sure soapy water does not get into his eyes or down his ears. When he is well sudded, rinse with plenty of warm water.

Hold a towel over him like an umbrella while he gives himself a really good shake. Then you can towel him down and he is ready to go.

If you are preparing your Stafford for a show, give him a bath a couple of days before the show rather than the night before as bathing often brings up dandruff. This is unsightly on the dog's coat – especially if he is dark-colored.

Don't over bathe your dog as you reduce the oils in his coat and these serve as protection against the weather.

Regular checks

When you get into a routine of grooming your Stafford on a regular basis, you can take the opportunity to examine him. This will allow you to spot any problems at any early stage.

Teeth

Start by examining your Stafford's teeth. While he is young his gums will be very sore during teething time, so be very gentle with his mouth. It is still a good idea to check his mouth as a Stafford can have what is termed 'converging' or 'in-growing' canines. This is where the large canine teeth on his bottom jaw are too far into the dog's mouth and do not clear the top ones. If this happens the canines can grow into the roof of the mouth.

Check when your puppy is losing his first teeth that the milk canines come out as the second ones come through. The second teeth might come up inside the baby ones, leaving the pup with two sets of these teeth. If you are concerned that this scenario is developing, consult your vet as he may decide to extract the milk teeth.

It is wise to clean your dog's teeth from an early age to prevent tooth decay later in his life. There are special dog toothpastes on the market which have flavours that are attractive to a dog. Alternatively you can buy chew-sticks which help to keep teeth clean.

Ears

Some Staffords suffer from ear problems, so it is a good idea to make sure your dog's ears are clean and free from odor. If his ears smell mousey consult you vet. Early action is best to avoid a deep-seated problem. Never poke cotton buds down into the ear canal.

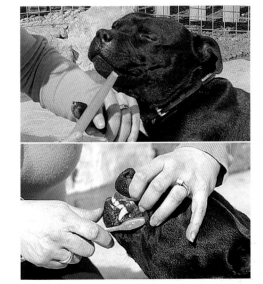

Nails can be kept in trim by using either a file or nail-clippers.

Regular brushing will keep the teeth clean and the gums healthy.

Nails

Walking on hard surfaces is essential to keep the nails in trim, but many Staffords will still need to have their nails trimmed.

It will pay dividends if you get your pup used to having his feet handled from the moment you bring him home. You don't have to do anything other than hold his paw, and look at his nails. This way, if you do have to cut his nails it will not be such a traumatic experience for him.

When you are cutting nails, put one arm firmly around him, lift his paw with the other hand and press lightly on his toes so that the nail is extended. This way you will be able to see where the quick of the nail begins. It is important that you avoid cutting into the quick as this will cause a great deal of bleeding. This is not dangerous but it is painful for the dog.

Exercising your Stafford

The Stafford is a very active dog, but he does not need miles of walking every day. Until he is at least nine months of age he will need a very moderate amount of exercise. Indeed, over-exercising at too early an age can harm his immature body. The main emphasis at this stage should be to introduce him to as many and as varied experiences as possible.

If you have to exercise your dog in a park, be sure to protect him from aggressive dogs. If you have the sort of Stafford that will not back down to the bully in the park, then be sensible and keep him on a lead near other dogs. No matter how much provocation you and your dog might have to endure, I can assure you that if your Stafford retaliates then he will always be blamed if a tussle ensues.

Fun and games

Because the Stafford is such an energetic, active dog, the very best sort of exercise for him is the violent type. The easiest way to provide this is to throw a ball. Make sure it is a hard ball and teach him to return it and give it up to you.

This is a hard lesson for a Stafford to learn as his instinct is to keep hold of his 'trophy'. He may be desperate to have the ball thrown again and again, but he cannot seem to resist the temptation to run off every time you want to take it from him. It may take some time for your dog to see the advantage of giving up his ball so that the game can continue, but the penny will drop in the end.

The older Stafford

As your Stafford gets older, his care requirements will change. If he is not taking as much exercise, he will not need the same volume of food. He may find it easier to cope with the same amount of food divided into two meals, given morning and evening.

If his digestion really starts to cause him problems, try changing his diet. There are commercial 'senior' diets on the market, which are easier to digest, or you could cook chicken and fish with rice for him. Many older Staffords suffer from arthritis and may need tablets or some form of additive to help their joints as they grow older.

If you take a young dog into the family, you may well find that the youngster gives your oldie a new lease of life. On the other hand, you must also guard against the old dog being ragged too much by the youngster.

Letting go

Inevitably the older dog will begin to fail. There are many medicines and procedures that vets can offer to prolong the life of an ageing dog, which is fine as long as the dog has some quality of life.

A dog that has been clean in the house all his life is distressed if he is unable to hold his water, and is fouling the house or his bed. A dog that is unable to walk far or enjoy exploring his surroundings through infirmity, cannot seek comfort in the television as a human might.

In the end we have to ask ourselves (and be brutally honest): are we keeping this dog alive for his sake or for our own? It is a terrible decision to make but one that nearly all dog owners and dog lovers have had to make at some time.

If you decide that it is time to let go, you can make things easier by asking the vet to make a home visit. This is, of course, very expensive. If you choose to take the dog into the surgery, be brave and stay with him until the end. Stroking and talking to your dog as he slips away is the last act of kindness you can do for him.

In time, you will be able to look back on all the happy times you shared with your beloved Stafford.

Socializing Staffords

The Staffordshire Bull Terrier is an outgoing, friendly dog, but he needs to learn the social skills to deal with different situations.

As a Stafford owner, it is your responsibility to provide him with learning opportunities. For your dog to enjoy a happy, well-balanced life, he needs:

- Knowledge of his place and role within his family.

- The ability to cope with the everyday situations he is likely to face during his lifetime.

The foundations for these are laid down from the time a puppy is born, but especially between the ages of four and ten weeks. For this reason, it is essential that breeders start the process of socialization – handling the puppies, getting them used to other people, other dogs, and the sounds of a household. You will need to continue and extend this program for the next 12 months and, indeed, throughout your Stafford's life.

Meeting people

A Stafford will continue to come into contact with new people. These may include your friends and relatives, the vet, other dog owners at training club, and, if they are to be shown, judges, stewards and other exhibitors. It is, therefore, important that your dog is confident with people in every situation.

Take your Stafford out and about, giving him the opportunity to meet and greet people of all ages in different environments.

It goes without saying that human contact should be positive and non-threatening.

Socializing with other dogs

In a variety of different situations I have seen the same scenario: a flustered Stafford owner tugging his snarling charge away from another dog – and the owner always says the same thing: "He's fine with my Staffs, he just hates other breeds."

He probably does not, or did not previously, hate all other breeds, but was either not exposed to them or had a bad experience with them during the socialization stage.

In an ideal world every Stafford would live in a multi-dog breed environment for the first three months of his life so that he receives maximum exposure to every form of canine – but clearly this is not feasible. Therefore we, as owners, must try to replicate as much of this dream situation as possible.

Getting it right

Do

- Attend socialization classes, especially if your puppy left his dam and siblings at an early age.

- Let your puppy socialize with other (vaccinated) dogs, but ensure your pup and the other dog(s) are on leads and supervised.

- Praise all positive interaction with other dogs.

- Try to expose your puppy to different ages, sizes and breeds of dogs.

- Ensure that exposure to other dogs is ongoing.

Don't

- Scoop your Stafford into your arms out of the way of a big dog's friendly, if overpowering, welcome. It will make the puppy fearful.

- Let your puppy off the lead with dogs you are unsure of.

- Introduce your pup to other dogs in their territory. Always choose somewhere away from beds or toys.

If a Stafford is well-socialized, he will not feel threatened and will respond in a positive manner.

Training guidelines

The characteristics of a Stafford – intelligence, eagerness to please and versatility – should make him an ideal candidate for training. He loves people, but unfortunately this eagerness to be friends with everyone can be one of the biggest barriers to learning.

How can a Stafford concentrate on one person telling him to "Stay" when there is a house full of other people who want to make a fuss of him?

How can he listen to his owner telling him to be "Steady" on the lead when the street is full of people he must meet and greet?

A Stafford puppy wriggling with glee is hard to resist, which is why it is important that the basics are learned in a more controlled situation before the big debut for the rest of the world.

Rule number one for training therefore is to ensure initial commands are learned in a suitably quiet and people free area where the puppy can concentrate on the learning process without distraction.

Other considerations should be:

- The time of day. If the puppy has run around all day he may be too tired for effective learning.

- When he had his last meal. Puppies with full stomachs are less likely to respond to treats.

- The mood of the trainer. If you have had a fractious day at work this may well affect your patience.

Benefits of training

Training your Staffordshire Bull Terrier has many benefits, including:

- Emphasizing the role of the owner in the household as the pack leader: The wolf terminology.

- Building a closer bond with the animal: Shared communication.

- Clearly defining hierarchies: You are training the animal therefore you are in charge – he is a lesser pack member.

- Mind stimulation: Staffords love learning new activities and being rewarded by praise and food.

Facing page:
Provide mental stimulation by teaching something new.

Dog Expert | 129

First lessons

Training should start from the moment your puppy arrives in his new home so that he begins to understand the behavior you want from him. But it is equally important to make training an enjoyable experience for both of you, interspersing teaching with play, praise and reward.

Wearing a collar

Puppies are usually introduced to their first collar at about eight weeks old.

First collars should be reasonably soft and easy to put on and remove. An owner fumbling with a stiff new buckle while the puppy is in effect trapped in their grasp is not the ideal way to introduce a puppy to training equipment.

The collar should only be left on for about 10 minutes the first time. The puppy will roll around and generally scratch at this alien item trying to remove it.

It is a good idea to distract his attention by feeding him or playing a game with him immediately after you have put the collar on.

Gradually increase the wearing time until the pup becomes accustomed to it – but do not leave it on when your puppy is in his crate. There have been accidents where the collar has got trapped in the bars of the crate.

Once he is totally comfortable with his collar, lead training – with a lightweight lead – can begin.

Lead training

For all of his little life to date, your puppy has been a free spirit, now all of a sudden he finds himself restrained. It is therefore important that he learns the benefit of the lead – being on the lead means he is close to his owner.

- Once the lead is attached to the collar, encourage the puppy to you and make a big fuss of him.

- Pick up the lead and step back until puppy is at the end of the lead and can just feel the pressure, then call him to you for fuss.

- Repeat until you are sure that the puppy is comfortable with you being at the far end of his lead, knowing he can access you easily.

- This exercise is sufficient for a first collar and lead experience. Repeat over the next couple of days but gradually try a gentle pull of the lead, encouraging the puppy towards you. The puppy should be happy

Facing page: The aim is for your Stafford to walk at your side – neither pulling ahead nor lagging behind.

to respond as he does not see the lead as a threat to his freedom but as a means to come close to you – and there is nowhere else he would rather be.

- If your puppy shows reluctance, revert to your original plan and call him over for fuss.

- Gentle perseverance and patience will ensure a happy puppy eager to trot on the lead beside you.

Come when called

This is an easy command to teach because a Stafford is only too keen to come to you for a fuss. However, it can become more problematic when distractions are added.

Hopefully, the breeder will have started the process by calling the puppies at mealtimes, and when ushering them in and out of their play area and sleeping quarters.

When your puppy arrives in his new home, he will feel a little lost and bewildered, and so he will want to follow you. Capitalise on this by calling his name and giving him a big fuss when he comes to you.

When he is responding every time you call, extend the distance by calling him in from the garden, or calling him from one room to another. Give him lots of praise and a treat, so he builds up a really positive association with the "Come" command.

Adding distractions

When you are out on a walk in the park, there are lots of temptations that lie in your Stafford 's path. There will be interesting scents, people to meet, and other dogs, so you need to make you have a reliable response to the "Come" command before putting it to the test.

The aim is to make yourself irresistible so your Stafford wants to come back to you. When you let him off lead, show him you have treats, and call him to you at regular intervals throughout the walk, giving him lots of praise and rewarding him. In this way, he learns that coming to you is always a good option.

If he is slow to respond, make yourself more exciting by using a high-pitched voice, jumping up and down, or even turning your back on him and running away a short distance.

Do not make the mistake of only calling your Stafford at the end of a walk. It will not take him long to realize that coming to you means having his lead clipped on, and the end of his free running fun. Keep your Stafford guessing by calling him at intervals throughout your walk, giving him a reward, and then letting him go free again.

If you do not think your Stafford is ready to free run, attach a training line to your Stafford's collar so

Facing page: Wait until you have a reliable recall before allowing your Stafford off-lead.

that he has freedom to roam, but you retain control. You can call him to you, giving a tug on the line if necessary, and then you will be able to reward him for coming to you.

This lesson is worth working at, for a Stafford who is allowed free running exercise will have a much better quality of life.

Stationary exercises

Consistency in commands and rewards combined with clear firm verbal communication should be what we all aim for when training our puppies.

Make sure that the command or cue words are adhered to – especially at the basic training stage – and that one word communicates to the puppy the action that is required.

Teaching "Sit"

This is an easy exercise to teach, and is one that you will use most often.

- Show your puppy you have a treat, and hold it just above his nose.

- As he looks up at the treat, he will lower his hindquarters going into the Sit position. Praise and reward him the moment he is in the correct position.

- Keep practising until your puppy understands what is required. You can then introduce the verbal cue, "Sit".

- You can reinforce this exercise at mealtimes, asking your puppy to "Sit" before you put his bowl down.

In time, you can withdraw the food lure and your puppy will respond to the verbal cue alone. However, it is a good idea to reward him on a random basis to keep him motivated. This applies to all training exercises.

Teaching "Down"

This is one of the most important exercises to teach. If your Stafford can respond instantly to the "Down" command, it could even prove to be a life-saver.

You can teach this from the Sit, or when your puppy is standing.

- Show your puppy you have a treat and slowly lower it to the ground, aiming for a spot between his front legs. Close your hand over the treat so he can't get it!

- As your puppy tries to get the treat, he will go into a bow, and then his hindquarters will follow so he is in the Down position. Praise and reward immediately he is in the correct position.

- Keep practising, and when your puppy understands the exercise, introduce the verbal cue, "Down".

- Work at extending the time your puppy stays in the Down before rewarding him.

Control exercises

The Stafford lives life in the fast lane so it is important you establish a measure of control to keep him safe. This may take a little time as you will need to curb his natural ebullience.

Teaching "Stay"

It may be easier to teach this exercise with your puppy on the lead to begin with. He can be in the Sit or Down position, although a Stafford is more likely to stay if he is in the Down.

- Stand in front of your puppy and take two paces backwards. Use a hand signal – palm facing towards your puppy – which effectively blocks his advance.

- Wait a couple of seconds and return to stand in front of your puppy. Release him with a cue such as "OK" and then praise and reward him.

- Keep practising before you introduce the verbal cue, "Stay".

- Work at increasing the distance and the amount of time you can leave your Stafford.

- It may take some time to build up a reliable "Stay", but it is well worth the effort.

Teaching "No" and "Leave"

The Stafford equivalent of the word "No" can be seen in the nursing bitch when a sharp-nailed, biting pup has overstepped the mark once too often on her over-suckled teats. It is effective and commands an instant cessation of the undesired activity, or it prevents an activity that is about to occur.

If "No" is used too often its impact is reduced. "No" should not mean: "you can't have that bone" nor should it mean: "stop mugging the visitors". "No" should be high impact.

The Stafford does not need to be given a reason for the "No" command but should instantly obey it. Tone of voice and the owner's natural body language in a "No" situation (generally thrust towards the puppy) evokes the response.

On other occasions, the "Leave" command can be used. "Leave" the bone (for the moment). "Leave" the toy (for later). Leave does not threaten nor suggest dire outcomes; it is a command to be obeyed like "Sit" and "Come" but it is part of the everyday communication between owner and Stafford.

"Leave" can be taught at an early age, but there does need to be a reward – a swap –for obedience. Returning to the wolf pack, imagine a newly weaned cub finding a sliver of meat left from the pack's feeding frenzy. The cub is not going to give up his prize easily. He will guard his morsel to the best of his capability. He will only be encouraged to part with it if there is a good game to be had with his siblings, a bigger slice of the kill from his mother, or the promise of a well-earned sleep.

Below: "Leave" means release the toy or bone without argument.

Therefore, when teaching "Leave", offer praise and fuss for what has been relinquished, or a treat or walk as a swap until the command is learned and becomes second nature, and is a willingly obeyed command.

Teaching "Wait"

In my experience, "Wait" is most easily learned by a Stafford when it is combined with other activities, such as playing in the garden.

There the "Wait" command can be given before a toy is thrown and the puppy has to stand in anticipation of the throw. "Wait" is used to command the puppy to stand still while a garden gate is being opened before going out for a walk, and "Wait" is said before crossing a busy road. "Wait" as a command can be used to control (generally), more so than any other command, because it is logical.

It indicates to the dog that nothing will occur unless the command is obeyed: the toy will not be thrown, the gate will not be opened, we will not cross the road. 'Wait' to a Stafford means: "wait for something to follow."

The ebullient Stafford

The Staffordshire Bull Terrier is powerful and compact, and he has an outstanding *joie de vivre*. This is an essential part of the Stafford charm – but when your Stafford launches himself like a cannonball when he comes to greet you, you feel the need to curb his enthusiasm.

Although you may not wish to dampen your Stafford's high spirits, there are times when his exuberance needs to be tempered. This is particularly the case if you are in the company of people who are elderly or frail, or with young children. The Stafford needs to learn that jumping up is not acceptable, and when you call 'time' on a game, he will calm down.

The strongest tool you have is ignoring your Stafford when he jumps up, or becomes too boisterous when he is playing. Simply suspend all activity, avoid eye

contact and turn your back on him. Initially, your Stafford will pester you, trying to force a reaction, but ignore him until he is quiet and has all four feet on the ground.

You can then praise him and reward him for the behavior you want. It is essential to be consistent so your Stafford understands that 'good' behavior is more rewarding than mugging you for attention.

Opportunities for Staffords

The Staffordshire Bull Terrier is an intelligent dog who will enjoy being given an outlet for his energy – both mentally and physically.

Good Citizen Scheme

A good starting point is the Good Citizen Scheme, run by the American Kennel Club in the USA and the Kennel Club in the UK. The aim is to promote responsible ownership and to train dogs to become model canine citizens. In the US there is one test; in the UK there are four award levels: Puppy Foundation, Bronze, Silver and Gold.

Agility

When looking at a mature Stafford standing foursquare, the term 'aerodynamic' does not instantly spring to mind. Yet Staffords are remarkably agile and fast when free-ranging. For the more active Stafford owner, agility is fun and ideal for the mental and

physical well-being of the dog. The set agility course is over a series of obstacles, which include:

- Jumps (upright and long)
- Weaving poles
- A-frame
- Dog walk
- Seesaw
- Tunnels

All of this is done at speed with the winner completing the course in the fastest time with the lowest faults. Penalties are incurred for missing the contact areas on the A-frame, dog walk or seesaw, and for refusals, missing weaves and knocking poles down. The dog and handler are eliminated for taking the wrong route. Agility dogs need to be fast, accurate and responsive to the handler's commands.

Obedience

Training your dog in formal obedience can range from regularly attending a training club to competing in competitive obedience shows where you progress through the levels from novice to advanced. Exercises include heelwork, recall, stays, retrieve, scent discrimination, send-away, and distance control.

Competitive obedience requires accuracy and precision, which may not suit the high-energy Stafford who likes to do everything with gusto, but he certainly has the brains for it.

Flyball

This is a team sport where dogs must clear a series of hurdles, retrieve a ball from the flyball box, and then return, clearing the hurdles for a second time, to cross the finishing line. It's fast, exciting – and very noisy! If you can get your Stafford addicted to a tennis ball, he will surprise you with just how fast he can move.

The show ring

To prepare for the show ring, you need to train your Stafford to stand in a show pose, to be examined by a judge, and to move correctly. Ringcraft classes will teach you how to do this, and will also give you a good grounding in show etiquette. It also provides an excellent opportunity to socialize your Stafford with other dogs.

Showing starts with small, informal shows and then progresses to bigger shows becoming increasingly competitive. The ambition of all those involved in showing is to make their dog a Champion.

Opposite: Flyball is fast... and noisy!

UP THE FLYERS!

Health care
for Staffords

Staffordshire Bull Terriers are stoical dogs with a good lifespan, which can run well into double figures provided their needs are met.

The Stafford is renowned as a plucky, faithful companion, with no physical exaggerations, so with good routine care, a well balanced diet, and sufficient exercise, most dogs will experience few health problems. However, it is your responsibility to put a program of preventative health care in place – and this should start from the moment your puppy, or older dog, arrives in his new home.

Vaccinations

Dogs are subject to a number of contagious diseases. In the old days, these were killers, and resulted in heartbreak for many owners. Vaccinations have now been developed, and the occurrence of the major infectious diseases is now

very rare. However, this will only remain the case if all pet owners follow a strict policy of vaccinating their dogs.

There are vaccinations available for the following diseases:

Adenovirus: This affects the liver; affected dogs have a classic 'blue eye'.

Distemper: A viral disease which causes chest and gastro-intestinal damage. The brain may also be affected, leading to fits and paralysis.

Parvovirus: Causes severe gastro enteritis, and most commonly affects puppies.

Leptospirosis: This bacterial disease is carried by rats and affects many mammals, including humans. It causes liver and kidney damage.

Rabies: A virus that affects the nervous system and is invariably fatal. The first signs are abnormal behavior when the infected dog may bite another animal or a person. Paralysis and death follow. Vaccination is compulsory in most countries. In the UK, dogs traveling overseas must be vaccinated.

Kennel Cough: There are several strains of Kennel Cough, but they all result in a harsh, dry, cough. This disease is rarely fatal; in fact most dogs make a good recovery within a matter of weeks and show few signs of ill health while they are affected. However, kennel cough is highly infectious among dogs that live together so, for this reason, most boarding kennels will insist that your dog is protected by the vaccine, which is given as nose drops.

Lyme Disease: This is a bacterial disease transmitted by ticks (see page 166). The first signs are limping, but the heart, kidneys and nervous system can also be affected. The ticks that transmit the disease occur in specific regions, such as the north-east states of the USA, some of the southern states, California and the upper Mississippi region. Lyme disease is still rare in the UK so vaccinations are not routinely offered.

Vaccination program

In the USA, the American Animal Hospital Association advises vaccination for core diseases, which they list as: distemper, adenovirus, parvovirus and rabies. The requirement for vaccinating for non-core diseases – leptospriosis, Lyme disease and kennel cough – should be assessed depending on a dog's individual risk and his likely exposure to the disease.

In the UK, vaccinations are routinely given for distemper, adenovirus, leptospirosis and parvovirus.

In most cases, a puppy will start his vaccinations at around eight weeks of age, with the second part given in a fortnight's time. However, this does vary depending on the individual policy of veterinary practices, and the incidence of disease in your area.

You should also talk to your vet about whether to give annual booster vaccinations. This depends on an individual dog's levels of immunity, and how long a particular vaccine remains effective.

Parasites

No matter how well you look after your Staffordshire Bull Terrier you will have to accept that parasites – internal and external – are ever present, and you need to take preventative action.

Internal parasites: As the name suggests, these parasites live inside your dog. Most will find a home in the digestive tract, but there is also a parasite that lives in the heart. If infestation is unchecked, a dog's health will be severely jeopardized, but routine preventative treatment is simple and effective.

External parasites: These parasites live on your dog's body – in his skin and fur, and sometimes in his ears.

Roundworm

This is found in the small intestine, and signs of infestation will be a poor coat, a pot belly, diarrhoea and lethargy. Pregnant mothers should be treated, but it is almost inevitable that parasites will be passed on to the puppies. For this reason, a breeder will start a worming program, which you will need to continue. Ask your vet for advice on treatment, which will need to continue throughout your dog's life.

Tapeworm

Infection occurs when fleas and lice are ingested; the adult worm takes up residence in the small intestine, releasing mobile segments (which contain eggs) which can be seen in a dog's feces as small rice-like grains. The only other obvious sign of infestation is irritation of the anus. Again, routine preventative treatment is required throughout your Stafford's life.

Heartworm

This parasite is transmitted by mosquitoes, and so will only occur where these insects thrive. A warm environment is needed for the parasite to develop, so it is more likely to be present in areas with a warm, humid climate. However, it is found in all parts of the USA, although its prevalence does vary. At present, heartworm is rarely seen in the UK.

Facing page: You will need to continue the worming program started by your puppy's breeder.

Heartworms live in the right side of the heart and larvae can grow up to 14 in (35 cm) in length. A dog with heartworm is at severe risk from heart failure, so preventative treatment, as advised by your vet, is essential. Dogs living in the USA should have regular blood tests to check for the presence of infection.

Lungworm

Lungworm, or *Angiostrongylus vasorum*, is a parasite that lives in the heart and major blood vessels supplying the lungs. It can cause many problems, such as breathing difficulties, excessive bleeding, sickness and diarrhoea, seizures, and can even be fatal. The parasite is carried by slugs and snails (and their trails), and the dog becomes infected when ingesting these, often accidentally when rummaging through undergrowth.

Lungworm is not common, but it is on the increase. Fortunately, it is easily preventable and even affected dogs usually make a full recovery if treated early enough. Your vet will be able to advise you on the risks in your area and what form of treatment may be required.

Fleas

A dog may carry dog fleas, cat fleas, and even human fleas. The flea stays on the dog only long enough to have a blood meal and to breed, but its

presence will result in itching and scratching. If your dog has an allergy to fleas – which is usually a reaction to the flea's saliva – he will scratch himself until he is raw.

Spot-on treatment, which should be administered on a routine basis, is easy to use and highly effective on all types of fleas. You can also treat your dog with a spray or with insecticidal shampoo. Bear in mind that the whole environment your dog lives in will need to be sprayed, and all other pets living in your home will also need to be treated.

How to detect fleas

You may suspect your dog has fleas, but how can you be sure? There are two methods to try.

Run a fine comb through your dog's coat, and see if you can detect the presence of fleas on the skin, or clinging to the comb. Alternatively, sit your dog on some white paper and rub his back. This will dislodge feces from the fleas, which will be visible as small brown specks. To double check, shake the specks on to some damp cotton-wool (cotton). Flea feces consists of the dried blood taken from the host, so if the specks turn a lighter shade of red, you know your dog has fleas.

Ticks

These are blood-sucking parasites which are most frequently found in rural areas where sheep or deer are present. The main danger is their ability to pass Lyme disease, which is prevalent in some areas of the USA (see page 158), although it is still rare in the UK. The treatment you give your dog for fleas generally works for ticks, but you should discuss the best product to use with your vet.

How to remove a tick

If you spot a tick on your dog, do not try to pluck it off as you risk leaving the hard mouth parts embedded. The best way to remove a tick is to use a fine pair of tweezers or you can buy a tick remover. Grasp the tick head firmly and then pull the tick straight out from the skin. If you are using a tick remover, check the instructions, as some recommend a circular twist when pulling. When you have removed the tick, clean the area with mild soap and water.

Ear mites

These parasites live in the outer ear canal. The signs of infestation are a brown, waxy discharge, and your dog will continually shake his head and scratch his ear. If you suspect your Stafford has ear mites, a visit to the vet will be needed so that medicated ear drops can be prescribed.

Fur mites

These small, white parasites are often referred to as 'walking dandruff'. They cause a scurfy coat and mild itchiness. However, they are zoonotic – transferable to humans – so prompt treatment with an insecticide prescribed by your vet is essential.

Harvest mites

These are picked up from the undergrowth, and can be seen as a bright orange patch on the webbing between the toes, although this can also be found elsewhere on the body, such as on the ear flaps. Treatment is effective with the appropriate insecticide.

Skin mites

There are two types of parasite that burrow into a dog's skin. Demodex canis is transferred from a mother to her pups while they are feeding. Treatment is with a topical preparation, and sometimes antibiotics are needed.

The other skin mite, sarcoptes scabiei, causes intense itching and hair loss. It is highly contagious. Treatment involves repeated bathing with a medicated shampoo.

Common ailments

As with all living animals, dogs can be affected by a variety of ailments, most of which can be treated effectively after consulting with your vet, who will prescribe appropriate medication and will advise you on how to care for your dog's needs.

Here are some of the more common problems that could affect your Staffordshire Bull Terrier, with advice on how to deal with them.

Anal glands

These are two small sacs on either side of the anus, which produce a dark-brown secretion that dogs use when they mark their territory. The anal glands should empty every time a dog defecates but, if they become blocked or impacted, a dog will experience increasing discomfort. He may nibble at his rear end, or 'scoot' his bottom along the ground to relieve the irritation.

Treatment involves a trip to the vet, who will empty the glands manually. It is important to do this without delay or infection may occur.

Dental problems

Good dental hygiene will do much to minimize problems with gum infection and tooth decay. If tartar accumulates to the extent that you cannot remove it by brushing, the vet will need to intervene. In a situation such as this, an anesthetic will need to be administered so the tartar can be removed manually.

Diarrhoea

There are many reasons why a dog has diarrhoea, but most commonly it is the result of scavenging, a sudden change of diet, or an adverse reaction to a particular type of food. The Stafford has a tough constitution, but digestive upset caused by scavenging is not unusual.

If your dog is suffering from diarrhoea, the first step is to withdraw food for a day. It is important that he does not dehydrate, so make sure that fresh drinking water is available. However, drinking too much can increase the diarrhoea, which may be accompanied with vomiting, so limit how much he drinks at any one time.

The Stafford is a natural scavenger and this may result in digestive upsets.

After allowing the stomach to rest, feed a bland diet, such as white fish or chicken with boiled rice, for a few days. In most cases, your dog's motions will return to normal and you can resume normal feeding, although this should be done gradually.

However, if this fails to work and the diarrhoea persists for more than a few days, you should consult your vet.

Your dog may have an infection, which needs to be treated with antibiotics, or the diarrhoea may indicate some other problem which needs expert diagnosis.

Ear infections

The Staffordshire Bill Terrier's ears are semi-pricked which allows air to circulate freely, but the breed can still be prone to ear infections.

A healthy ear is clean, with no sign of redness or inflammation, and no evidence of a waxy brown discharge or a foul odor. If you see your dog scratching his ear, shaking his head, or holding one ear at an odd angle, you will need to consult your vet.

The most likely causes are ear mites (see page 168), an infection, or there may a foreign body, such as a grass seed, trapped in the ear (see page 176).

Depending on the cause, treatment is with medicated ear drops, possibly containing antibiotics. If a foreign body is suspected, the vet will need to carry out further investigations.

Eye problems

The Stafford's eyes are positioned at the front of the head and there are neither bulbous nor deep-set exaggerations that can cause problems.

However, if your Stafford's eyes look red and sore, he may be suffering from conjunctivitis. This may, or may not be accompanied with a watery or a crusty discharge. Conjunctivitis can be caused by a bacterial or viral infection, it could be the result of an injury, or it could be an adverse reaction to pollen.

You will need to consult your vet for a correct diagnosis, but in the case of an infection, treatment with medicated eye drops is effective.

Conjunctivitis may also be the first sign of more serious inherited eye problems (see page 184).

Foreign bodies

In the home, puppies – and some older dogs – cannot resist chewing anything that looks interesting. This is most particularly true of the Stafford who has a somewhat destructive turn of mind.

The toys you choose for your dog should be suitably robust to withstand damage, but some dogs will chew – and swallow – anything from socks, tights, and other items from the laundry basket, to golf balls and stones from the garden. Obviously, these items are indigestible and could cause an obstruction in your dog's intestine, which is potentially lethal.

The signs to look for are vomiting, and a tucked up posture. The dog will often be restless and will look as though he is in pain. In this situation, you must get your dog to the vet without delay as surgery will be needed to remove the obstruction.

The other type of foreign body that may cause problems is grass seed. A grass seed can enter an orifice such as a nostril, down an ear, the gap between the eye and the eyelid, or penetrate the soft skin between the toes. It can also be swallowed.

The introduction of a foreign body induces a variety of symptoms, depending on the point of entry and where it travels to. The signs to look for include head shaking/ ear scratching, the eruption of an abscess, sore, inflamed eyes, or a persistent

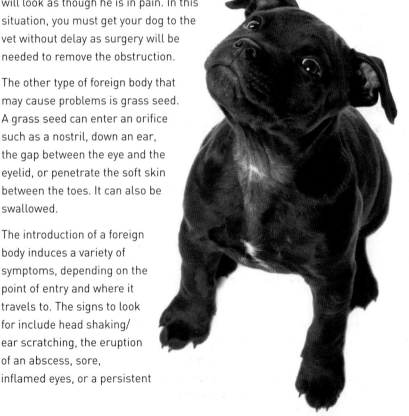

cough. The vet will be able to make a proper diagnosis, and surgery may be required.

Heatstroke

The Staffordshire Bull Terrier is a hardy breed but care should be taken on hot days as heatstroke is a potential danger. When the temperature rises, make sure your dog always has access to shady areas, and wait for a cooler part of the day before going for a walk. Be extra careful if you leave your Stafford in the car, as the temperature can rise dramatically – even on a cloudy day. Heatstroke can happen very rapidly, and unless you are able lower your dog's temperature, it can be fatal.

If your Stafford appears to be suffering from heatstroke, lie him flat and try to reduce his core body temperature by wrapping him in cool towels. A dog should not be immersed in cold water as this will cause the blood vessels to constrict, impeding heat dissipation. As soon as he made some recovery, take him to the vet, where cold intravenous fluids can be administered.

Lameness/ limping

There are a wide variety of reasons why your Stafford could go lame. These range from a simple muscle strain to more serious problems such as a fracture or ligament damage. Sometimes there may be more complex issues with the joints, which may be due to an inherited disorder.

The Stafford is a powerhouse of energy; he has a tendency to literally throw himself into activities, so minor injuries can occur. However, it takes an expert to make a correct diagnosis, so if you are concerned about your dog, do not delay in seeking help.

As your Stafford becomes elderly, he may suffer from arthritis, which you will see as general stiffness, particularly when he gets up after resting. It will help if you ensure his bed is in a warm, draught-free location, and, if your Stafford gets wet after exercise, you must dry him thoroughly.

If your elderly Stafford seems to be in pain, consult your vet who will be able to help with pain relief medication.

Skin problems

If your dog is scratching or nibbling at his skin, the first thing to check for is fleas (see page 164). There are other external parasites which cause itching and hair loss, but you will need a vet to help you find the culprit.

An allergic reaction is another major cause of skin problems. It can be quite an undertaking to find the cause of the allergy, and you will need to follow your vet's advice, which often requires eliminating specific ingredients from the diet, as well as looking at environmental factors.

Pain Threshold

Staffords are notoriously tough and can keep going in spite of extreme illness or pain. It is important for the Stafford owner to be aware of this because of the danger of misinterpreting signs of ill health or injury. If you have any concerns over your Staffrd's health, do not delay in seeking expert advice.

Inherited disorders

Like all pedigree dogs, the Staffordshire Bull Terrier does have a few breed-related disorders. The diseases in this chapter can affect offspring so breeding from affected dogs should be discouraged. Although breeders strive to eliminate these problems, it is important to research thoroughly before buying a puppy.

There are now recognized screening tests to enable breeders to check for affected individuals and hence reduce the prevalence of these diseases within the breed. DNA testing is also becoming more widely available, and as research into the different genetic diseases progresses, more DNA tests are being developed.

Elbow and hip dysplasia

These are inherited orthopedic disorders which show a spectrum of changes, and can be crippling. There is instability of the malformed joints, such that arthritis develops in an attempt to achieve better stability but may simply contribute to, or worsen, the level of pain.

The degree of change seen radiographically is not necessarily a good guide to the effect on the individual: a dog with a very high hip score may not be as lame as a dog with a lower one, hence the need for a standardised scoring/grading system.

In the US, X-rays are submitted to the Orthopedic Foundation for Animals; in the UK X-rays are sent to the British Veterinary Association. Severely affected dogs should not be used for breeding.

Eye conditions

There are a couple of eye conditions to be aware of.

Hereditary and juvenile cataracts

This is not a congenital condition. There is juvenile-onset of progressive development of cataracts in the lenses of both eyes, commonly quoted as starting at five to eight months of age, but which may actually be detected as early as three or four weeks.

Affected individuals will be total blind by the age of between one and three years. Carriers can now be identified with a DNA test.

Persistent Hyperplastic Primary Vitreous (PHPV)

Affected individuals retain the developmental blood supply to the lens to a varying degree in one or both eyes. Since these vessel remnants lie within the line of vision, sight will be affected to a variable degree. Fortunately, it can be so mild as to cause no sight impairment. PHPV is not in itself progressive, although blindness can result from hemorrhage within the eye and cataract formation. The mode of inheritance involved in PHPV is unclear. Since it is a congenital fault, present at birth, puppies can be examined and affected individuals identified from six weeks of age.

L-2-Hydroxyglutaric Aciduria (L2-HGA)

This is a so-called metabolic disorder with serious, distressing consequences. There is a wide range of signs which may be shown by an affected individual. These include behavioral changes and dementia (for example, staring blankly at the wall, or becoming so disorientated and confused by his surroundings as to become marooned under a table or in a corner of the room), anxiety attacks, reduced ability to exercise, wobbly gait (ataxia) and muscular stiffness, tremors or full seizures (so it can be mistaken for epilepsy).

It is inherited as an autosomal recessive, meaning that both parents must be carriers (or affected) for an individual to manifest the disorder. A DNA test is now available to identify carriers to ensure they are only bred to clear individuals which will avoid the production of affected offspring.

Overlong soft palate

This is considered hereditary and does occur in other brachycephalic breeds such as the Bulldog and Pekingese. It is seen only rarely in the Stafford, suggested by some to be a reflection of his more pronounced vertical 'stop', although a cluster occurred a few years ago in related Staffords.

Patellar luxation

This is the condition where the kneecap or patella slips out of position, locking the knee or stifle so that it will not bend and causing the characteristic hopping steps until the patella slips back into its position over the stifle joint. Fortunately, it is not very common in the Stafford. Surgical correction is possible in severely affected dogs.

Summing up

It may give the pet owner cause for concern to find about health problems that may affect their dog. But it is important to bear in mind that acquiring some basic knowledge is an asset, as it will allow you to spot signs of trouble at an early stage. Early diagnosis is very often the means to the most effective treatment.

Fortunately, the Stafford is a generally healthy dog with his only visits to the vet being annual check-ups. In most cases, owners can look forward to enjoying many happy years with this loyal companion.

Facing page:
With good care and management, your Stafford should live a long and healthy life.

Useful addresses

Breed & Kennel Clubs
Please contact your Kennel Club to obtain
contact information about breed clubs in
your area.

UK
The Kennel Club (UK)
1 Clarges Street London, W1J 8AB
Telephone: 0870 606 6750
Fax: 0207 518 1058
Web: www.thekennelclub.org.uk

USA
American Kennel Club (AKC)
5580 Centerview Drive, Raleigh, NC 27606.
Telephone: 919 233 9767
Fax: 919 233 3627
Email: info@akc.org
Web: www.akc.org

United Kennel Club (UKC)
100 E Kilgore Rd, Kalamazoo,
MI 49002-5584, USA.
Tel: 269 343 9020
Fax: 269 343 7037
Web:www.ukcdogs.com/

Australia
Australian National Kennel Council (ANKC)
The Australian National Kennel Council is
the administrative body for pure breed canine
affairs in Australia. It does not, however,
deal directly with dog exhibitors, breeders
or judges. For information pertaining to
breeders, clubs or shows, please contact the
relevant State or Territory Body.

International
Fédération Cynologique Internationalé (FCI)
Place Albert 1er, 13, B-6530 Thuin, Belgium.
Tel: +32 71 59.12.38
Fax: +32 71 59.22.29
Web: www.fci.be/

Training and behavior
UK
Association of Pet Dog Trainers
Telephone: 01285 810811
Web: http://www.apdt.co.uk

Association of Pet Behavior Counsellors
Telephone: 01386 751151
Web: http://www.apbc.org.uk/

USA
Association of Pet Dog Trainers
Tel: 1 800 738 3647
Web: www.apdt.com/

American College of Veterinary Behaviorists
Web: http://dacvb.org/

American Veterinary Society of Animal
Behavior
Web: www.avsabonline.org/

Australia
APDT Australia Inc
Web: www.apdt.com.au

Canine Behavior
For details of regional behaviorists, contact
the relevant State or Territory Controlling
Body.

Activities

UK

Agility Club
http://www.agilityclub.co.uk/

British Flyball Association
Telephone: 01628 829623
Web: http://www.flyball.org.uk/

USA

North American Dog Agility Council
Web: www.nadac.com/

North American Flyball Association, Inc.
Tel/Fax: 800 318 6312
Web: www.flyball.org/

Australia

Agility Dog Association of Australia
Tel: 0423 138 914
Web: www.adaa.com.au/

NADAC Australia (North American Dog
Agility Council - Australian Division)
Web: www.nadacaustralia.com/

Australian Flyball Association
Tel: 0407 337 939
Web: www.flyball.org.au/

International

World Canine Freestyle Organisation
Tel: (718) 332-8336
Web: www.worldcaninefreestyle.org

Health

UK

British Small Animal Veterinary Association
Tel: 01452 726700
Web: http://www.bsava.com/

Royal College of Veterinary Surgeons
Tel: 0207 222 2001
Web: www.rcvs.org.uk

Alternative Veterinary Medicine Centre
Tel: 01367 710324
Web: www.alternativevet.org/

USA

American Veterinary Medical Association
Tel: 800 248 2862
Web: www.avma.org

American College of Veterinary Surgeons
Tel: 301 916 0200
Toll Free: 877 217 2287
Web: www.acvs.org/

Canine Eye Registration Foundation
The Veterinary Medical DataBases
1717 Philo Rd, PO Box 3007,
Urbana, IL 61803-3007
Tel: 217-693-4800
Fax: 217-693-4801
Web: http://www.vmdb.org/cerf.html

Orthopedic Foundation of Animals
2300 E Nifong Boulevard
Columbia, Missouri, 65201-3806
Tel: 573 442-0418
Fax: 573 875-5073
Web: http://www.offa.org/

American Holistic Veterinary Medical
Association
Tel: 410 569 0795
Web: www.ahvma.org/

Australia

Australian Small Animal Veterinary
Association
Tel: 02 9431 5090
Web: www.asava.com.au

Australian Veterinary Association
Tel: 02 9431 5000
Web: www.ava.com.au

Australian College Veterinary Scientists
Tel: 07 3423 2016
Web: http://acvsc.org.au

Australian Holistic Vets
Web: www.ahv.com.au/